SQUIRREL IS SAD • HIPPO IS HAPPY • SHEEP IS SCARED

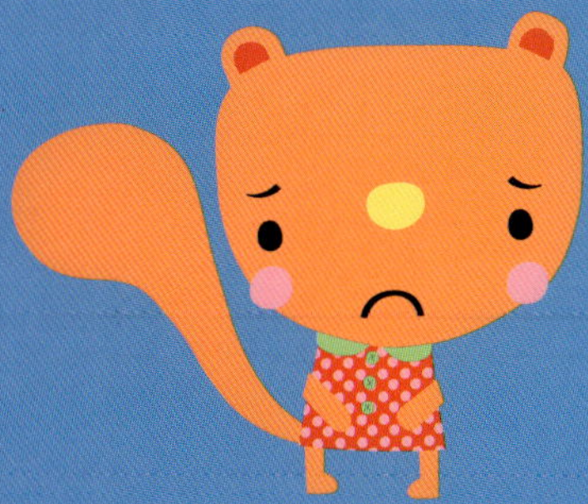

GOD
LOVES ME ALWAYS

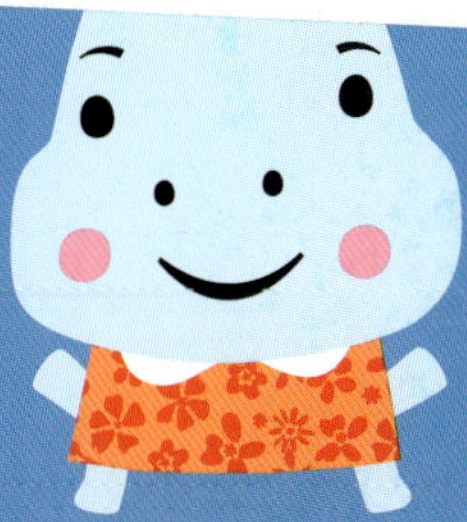

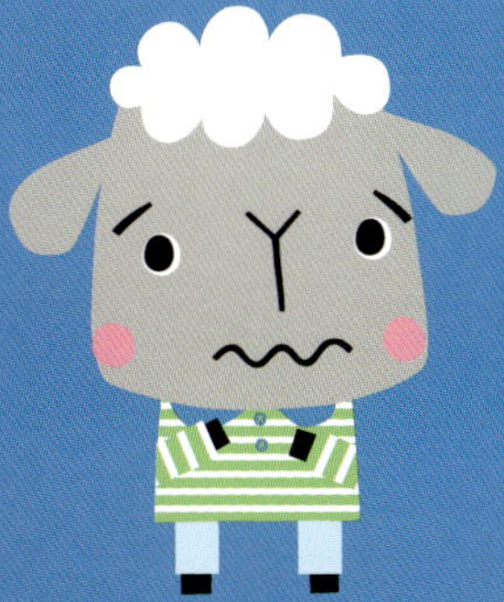

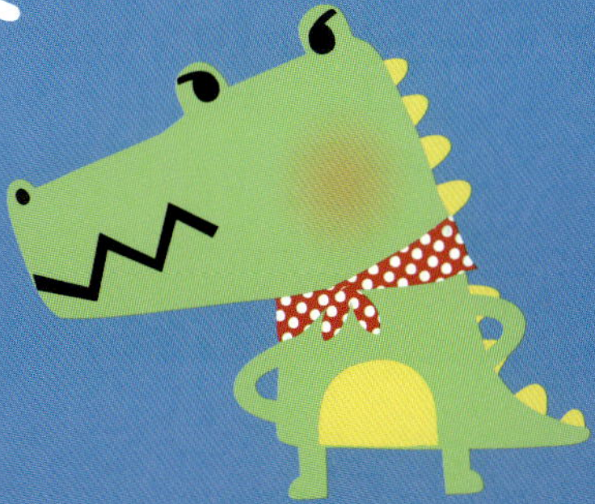

This collection of stories is the perfect introduction to emotions for young children. Through the Playdate Pals characters, children can learn how to recognise and respond to their emotions. There is also a reward chart with stickers to encourage and guide children on their emotional journey with God.

At the end of each story, you will find notes, questions and a verse from the Bible to encourage further discussion.

Rosie Greening • Dawn Machell

Squirrel's favourite toy was a small, brown bear.

His name was Ted.

Squirrel took Ted everywhere:

on walks . . .

up trees . . .

One day, **Squirrel** wanted to play with Ted.

She searched

and searched,

but she couldn't find Ted anywhere!

and baths were **no fun**!

Squirrel didn't feel like **doing anything** without Ted.

That night, there was a **Ted-shaped space** in **Squirrel's** bed.

She felt **lonely** and couldn't sleep, so she **curled** up in a ball and **hugged** her knees.

The next day, all the animals were playing together.

Puppy said, "Let's make a den for our favourite toys!"

Alligator saw **Squirrel** looking **sad**.

He said, "Let's make a Lost and Found poster for Ted. Then if someone finds Ted, they can give Ted back to you!"

Squirrel thought that was a great idea.

Squirrel drew Ted on a big piece of paper. Alligator wrote "Lost Bear" at the top.

Then they stuck the poster on the wall.

When Kitten saw the poster, she said, "I've seen that bear!"

She took **Squirrel** to the dressing-up box.

Ted was inside!

Squirrel thanked Kitten and Alligator, and then she gave Ted a big **hug**.

She felt **happy** to have such **helpful** friends, and she didn't feel **sad** anymore!

READING TOGETHER

Squirrel is Sad is designed to help children recognise their own feelings of sadness and how they might behave when they are sad. Once you have read the story together, go back and talk about any experiences the children might share with Squirrel.

Also talk about what the Bible has to say about **sadness:**

I am sad and tired. Make me strong again as you have promised.
Psalms 119:28 (ICB)

Explain that the Holy Spirit can remind us of this truth. He can also help us to respond to our emotions in ways that please God, so that we are not ruled by our emotions. Emotions are real, but they are not always good leaders. The Holy Spirit is the best leader.

Look at the pictures

Talk about the characters. Are they smiling, frowning, hiding or jumping? Help children think about what people look like or how they move their bodies when they are **sad.**

Words in bold

Throughout each story there are words highlighted in bold type. These words specify either the **character's name** or useful words and phrases relating to feeling **sadness.** You may wish to put emphasis on these words or use them as reminders for parts of the story you can return to and discuss.

Questions you can ask

To encourage further exploration of this feeling, you could try asking children some of the following questions:

- What makes you feel **sad** and how do you show it?
- When you are **sad,** what does it feel like in your body?
- What do you feel like doing when you are **sad?**
- What does the Bible teach us about **sadness?**

PLAYDATE PALS

Hippo is HAPPY

Rosie Greening • Dawn Machell

One day, Puppy saw **Hippo** looking **sad**, so he gave her an empty book with a big, **smiley** face on it.

"Why don't you fill it with things that make you **happy**?" suggested Puppy. **Hippo** opened the book and started to think.

First, **Hippo** thought about **playing** in the park.

"I **love** splashing around with my friends!" she thought.

Then **Hippo** thought about **playing** with her favourite toys – that made her **happy** too!

Hippo imagined **eating** ice cream and her tummy gave a rumble.

"Ice cream makes me **really happy**!" **giggled** Hippo.

After that, **Hippo** thought about getting a big **hug**.

"**Hugs** always make me **happy**.
And I **love** giving them too!" she thought.

Finally, **Hippo** thought about falling **asleep** in her bed.

"My bed is so cosy!"

"I feel **happy** and **safe** when I'm in bed," thought **Hippo**.

Hippo had lots of ideas, so Puppy offered to help her put them in the book.

They had lots of **fun** drawing together and that made **Hippo happy** too!

When the book was full, **Hippo** added stickers to make it look extra special.

"**Hooray**! My book is finished!" said **Hippo**, and she **jumped** with **excitement**.

Hippo and Puppy looked through the book together. "What a lovely book!" said Puppy.

Hippo felt a warm, **tingly** feeling in her tummy and she gave a big **smile**.

Being **friends** with Puppy made her **happiest** of all!

READING TOGETHER

Hippo is Happy is designed to help children recognise their own feelings of happiness and how they might behave when they are happy. Once you have read the story together, go back and talk about any experiences the children might share with Hippo.

Also talk about what the Bible has to say about **happiness:**

> **The Lord has done great things for us, and we are very glad.**
> *Psalms 126:3 (ICB)*

Explain that the Holy Spirit can remind us of this truth. He can also help us to respond to our emotions in ways that please God, so that we are not ruled by our emotions. Emotions are real, but they are not always good leaders. The Holy Spirit is the best leader.

Look at the pictures

Talk about the characters. Are they smiling, frowning, hiding or jumping? Help children think about what people look like or how they move their bodies when they are **happy.**

Words in bold

Throughout each story there are words highlighted in bold type. These words specify either the **character's name** or useful words and phrases relating to feeling **happiness.** You may wish to put emphasis on these words or use them as reminders for parts of the story you can return to and discuss.

Questions you can ask

To encourage further exploration of this feeling, you could try asking children some of the following questions:

- What makes you feel **happy** and how do you show it?
- When you are **happy,** what does it feel like in your body?
- What do you feel like doing when you are **happy?**
- What does the Bible teach us about **happiness?**

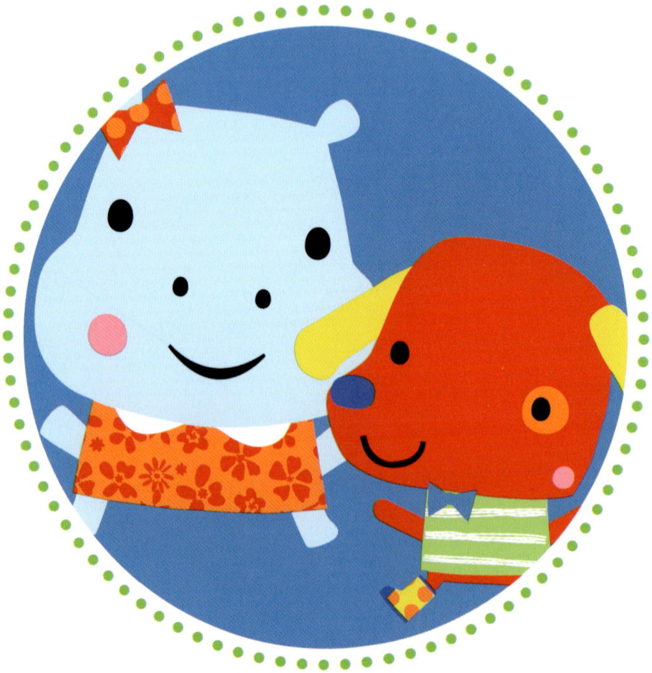

PLAYDATE PALS

Sheep is SCARED

Rosie Greening • Dawn Machell

Sheep was feeling **tired**.

He had been playing with his friends all day, and it was time for bed.

One by one, **Sheep's** friends fell asleep.

First Hippo...

then Alligator...

then Squirrel...

but Sheep was **wide awake.**

Sheep looked around. Everything seemed **different** in the dark.

The beds looked different, the room sounded different, and worst of all, **Sheep felt different**.

His heart began **beating** very hard and he started to **shake**.

Sheep saw something under Hippo's bed.
It was big, dark and **monster-shaped**!

"Oh, no! Maybe there is a monster under my bed too!" **whispered** Sheep, and he **hugged** his blanket tightly.

Suddenly, there was a loud **BANG**!

The **noise** made **Sheep jump**, and his tummy felt all **squiggly**.

"It's the monster!"
yelped Sheep.

Hippo heard **Sheep** and woke up.
Then Hippo turned on the light.

Sheep felt a little less **scared** now that the room looked normal again, but he didn't want to **let go** of his blanket.

"What's the matter, **Sheep**?" asked Hippo.

Sheep told them about the monster and his friends looked under Hippo's bed.

It wasn't a monster –
it was Hippo's boots!

Then **Sheep** remembered the **banging noises**.

Hippo opened the curtains.
It wasn't a monster – it was a storm!

The thunder **BOOMED** and **Sheep jumped.**

Hippo **hugged** Sheep. "Don't worry, **Sheep.** Everyone gets **scared** sometimes, but we'll look after you."

After that, **Sheep** felt a lot **happier**, so the friends went back to bed.

This time, **Sheep** had no trouble getting to sleep!

When **Sheep** woke up the next morning, he felt **happy** and **safe**.

The sun was shining, so the animals put on their boots and went outside.

The rain had made some lovely puddles to jump in!

Sheep had lots of **fun** playing with his friends.

READING TOGETHER

Sheep is Scared is designed to help children recognise their own feelings of fear and how they might behave when they are frightened. Once you have read the story together, go back and talk about any experiences the children might share with Sheep.

Also talk about what the Bible has to say about **fear**:

> Where God's love is, there is no fear, because God's perfect love takes away fear.
>
> 1 John 4:18a (ICB)

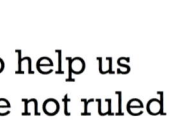

Explain that the Holy Spirit can remind us of this truth. He can also help us to respond to our emotions in ways that please God, so that we are not ruled by our emotions. Emotions are real, but they are not always good leaders. The Holy Spirit is the best leader.

Look at the pictures

Talk about the characters. Are they smiling, frowning, hiding or jumping? Help children think about what people look like or how they move their bodies when they are **scared.**

Words in bold

Throughout each story there are words highlighted in bold type. These words specify either the **character's name** or useful words and phrases relating to feeling **scared.** You may wish to put emphasis on these words or use them as reminders for parts of the story you can return to and discuss.

Questions you can ask

To encourage further exploration of this feeling, you could try asking children some of the following questions:

- What makes you feel **scared** and how do you show it?
- When you are **scared,** what does it feel like in your body?
- What do you feel like doing when you are **scared?**
- What does the Bible teach us about **fear?**

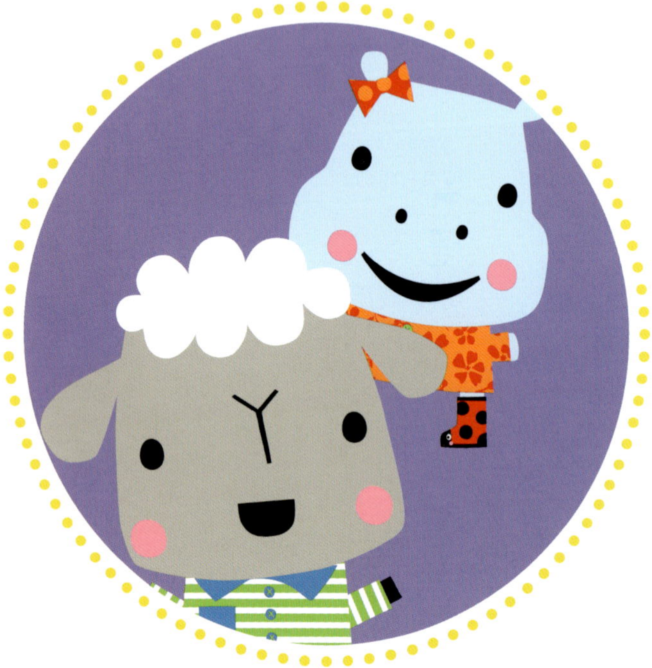

PLAYDATE PALS

Alligator is
ANGRY

Rosie Greening • Dawn Machell

It was a dark, rainy day and Bear and **Alligator** were deciding what to play.

"I know, let's paint some colourful flowers to brighten up this room!" said Bear.

"Good idea!" said **Alligator**.

The friends ran to get their aprons.

Alligator wanted the red apron, but Bear took it first.

"That's mine!" thought **Alligator**.
He **clenched** his teeth,
starting to feel **angry**.

Next, the animals went to the art table. Bear sat so close to **Alligator** that their pictures touched.

"Move over!" snapped **Alligator**, and he **pushed** Bear away.

Soon, **Alligator** was painting
a big, yellow flower.
He was just finishing the last petal
when Bear took the yellow paint.

"I need that!" thought **Alligator**, and his face started to get **hot**.

Alligator looked at his painting. He didn't like it, and the more he looked at it, the **hotter** and **angrier** he felt.

"I **want** the yellow paint!" exploded **Alligator**.

He **grabbed** the paint and it spilt over both paintings!

"My painting is ruined!" yelled **Alligator**. He felt a rush of **hot anger** burst out of his body.

He reached forward angrily
and **pinched** Bear!

Alligator ran away from the table. His heart was **beating fast** and he was **breathing hard**.

But when he looked back,
he saw that Bear was **crying**.

Alligator took a **deep breath** and started to **calm** down. He didn't like seeing Bear cry. It made him **feel bad**.

Alligator went back to the table and said, "I'm **sorry**, Bear. I didn't mean to make you **sad**."

"That's ok, I get **angry** sometimes too," said Bear, and they started painting a picture together.

They **shared** the table and took it in turns to use the yellow paint.

When Bear and **Alligator** had finished their painting, they stuck it on the wall.

It was beautiful and it filled the room with colour!

READING TOGETHER

Alligator is Angry is designed to help children recognise their own feelings of anger and how they might behave when they are angry. Once you have read the story together, go back and talk about any experiences the children might share with Alligator.

Also talk about what the Bible has to say about **anger**:

> **A foolish person loses his temper.**
> **But a wise person controls his anger.**
> *Proverbs 29:11 (ICB)*

Explain that the Holy Spirit can remind us of this truth. He can also help us to respond to our emotions in ways that please God, so that we are not ruled by our emotions. Emotions are real, but they are not always good leaders. The Holy Spirit is the best leader.

Look at the pictures

Talk about the characters. Are they smiling, frowning, hiding or jumping? Help children think about what people look like or how they move their bodies when they are **angry.**

Words in bold

Throughout each story there are words highlighted in bold type. These words specify either the **character's name** or useful words and phrases relating to feeling **anger.** You may wish to put emphasis on these words or use them as reminders for parts of the story you can return to and discuss.

Questions you can ask

To encourage further exploration of this feeling, you could try asking children some of the following questions:

- What makes you feel **angry** and how do you show it?
- When you are **angry,** what does it feel like in your body?
- What do you feel like doing when you are **angry?**
- What does the Bible teach us about **anger?**

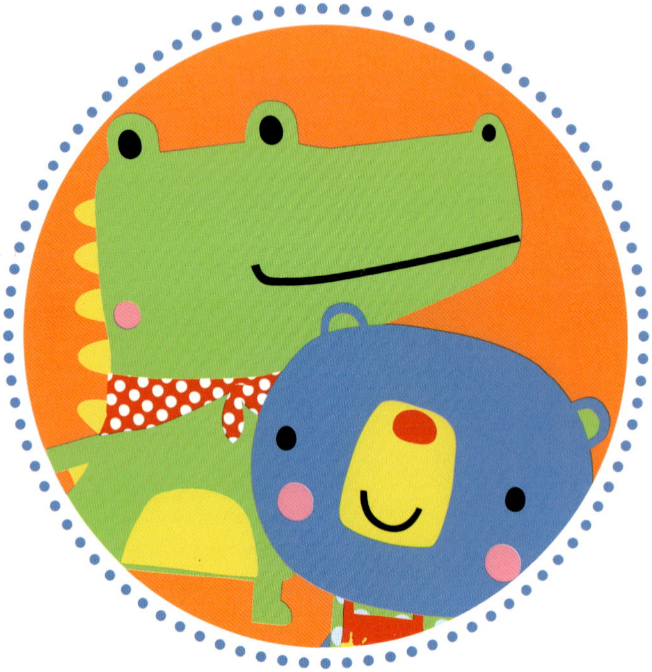